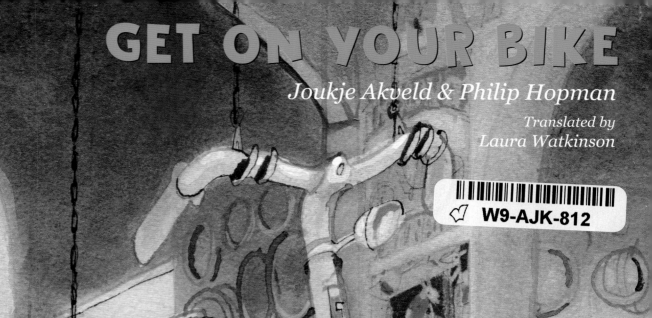

GET ON YOUR BIKE

Joukje Akveld & Philip Hopman

Translated by
Laura Watkinson

Eerdmans Books for Young Readers

Grand Rapids, Michigan

Bobby and William were having an argument.
It went a bit like this:
"Just for once, why can't you . . . !"
"Why do you always have to keep on . . . !"
"You don't think I'd ever . . . !"
And then someone said something about "spoiled."
Something flew through the air, but it didn't hit anyone.
William shouted, "Go on! Just get on your bike and leave!"

So that's what Bobby did.
There was a thundercloud in his head.
Lightning flashed between his ears.

Where should I go? thought Bobby.
The light straight ahead was green.
"Straight ahead," Bobby said.

Bobby biked down a long road.
Angry words crashed around inside his head.
That William. That buffle-brained William!

Now and then he passed a tree. Or a house.
Then there was nothing for a while.
Except for someone selling ice cream.

He came to a big intersection.
Where should I go now? thought Bobby.
The light for left was green.
"Left," Bobby said.

He was still thinking about pudding-headed William.
But the sun was shining. And a bird was singing too.

Bobby biked along a busy road.
Cars were whizzing by.
All around him, there was honking and hooting
and hollering.

He came to a barrier with a red light beside it.
Where should I go now? thought Bobby.
The light turned green and the barrier lifted.
"Straight ahead," Bobby said.

For the longest time, Bobby stood still.
In every direction he saw cars and trucks.
Vans and double-decker buses. Mopeds and bicycles.

He wasn't thinking about William anymore. William was stored away inside the junk room in his head with all the other things he never thought about. Scribbled-out drawings. The broken kite that wouldn't fly. William's flat bike tire. What he was thinking about now was the other side of the water and where to go and what to do next.

Bobby discovered that the other side of the water looked just like
his own side, only emptier. Here and there he saw a house.
Now and then he passed a tree. There were more frogs, though.
And perhaps the sun was shining a little more brightly.
But the grass over here was just as green.

Where should I go now? thought Bobby.
Then he heard a noise behind him.
It sounded like lots and lots of bike tires whooshing down the road.

Bobby looked over his shoulder.
It *was* lots and lots of bike tires whooshing
down the road.

After they'd all passed him, Bobby thought:
I wonder how William's doing.
Is he still angry with me?
Bobby wasn't nearly as angry as before.
And now he was hungry.

Bobby pedaled on for a while.
At the next intersection the left light
was green—and the one after that too.
He thought about what William had said.
Hmm, maybe sometimes I could . . .
he thought to himself.
And maybe I shouldn't always keep on . . .

Beneath him, the water flowed.
The right-turn light was green.

Bobby came to a long road.
He started pedaling faster. The wind helped him a bit.
A long stretch of nothing flashed by in no time at all.
The trees and houses had never whizzed by so quickly.

William was waiting at the door.
"I've been thinking about it, and perhaps I could . . ." he began.
He scratched his head and looked a bit embarrassed.
"Never mind," said Bobby. "I was actually thinking something like that myself."

They went inside and had dinner at the kitchen table.
"It nearly did get spoiled, though," said William. "And it's cold now too."
Bobby just smiled.
Tomorrow, he thought, *we'll get on our bikes and go for a ride together.*